DART
COUNTRY

featuring the area in and around
Stoke Gabriel, Churston, Kingswear and Galmpton

Deryck Sey

OBELISK PUBLICATIONS

Also by Deryck Seymour:
The Ghosts of Torbay
The Ghosts of Berry Pomeroy Castle
The Magic Triangle (South of the Teign Estuary)
A Secret Circle

We have over 160 Devon titles; for current list please send SAE to
Obelisk Publications, 2 Church Hill, Pinhoe, Exeter EX4 9ER

ACKNOWLEDGEMENTS

One of the pleasures of research is the fact that it brings one into contact with so many new acquaintances. As I explored "Dart Country" I made several new friends who helped me in one way or another. Particularly would I thank for their assistance: B. Baker, N. Betts, A. Bibby, C. Bircham, G. Bush, J. Collinson, A. Day, V. Duker, P. Folca, A. Grey, Miss Hotblack, Wendy Liscombe, Mrs C. G. Neill, Mr & Mrs Perman, P. Riley, Mr Rocksborough, D. Rowe, Miss A. Simpson, G. E. Smales, C. Smart, P. Varney, Mrs Vallance, J. W. Webber, P. Williams, Lt. Col. Willoughby, M.C., The Landmark Trust, The Devon Record Office, the helpful staff at Torquay Library, my ever-willing driver J. B. Hopwood and the script readers Mr J. Lawrence and Mrs E. Jerrard.

I do apologise if I have forgotten anyone.

Plate Acknowledgements
Chips Barber for all photographs.

BIBLIOGRAPHY
The Buildings of England – Devon, Hoskins; *The King's England – Devon*, Arthur Mee; *Dictionary of National Biography*; *The Exchequer Cartulary of Torre Abbey*; *Historic Dart*, Hemery; *The Newton Abbot to Kingswear Railway 1844–1988*; C. R. Potts; *Kingswear and Neighbourhood*, Russell and Yorke; *Guide to the Church of St Mary and St Gabriel; Stoke Gabriel, Guide to the Church of St Mary the Virgin, Churston Ferrers*, B. G. W. Burr; *Guide to the church of St Thomas of Canterbury, Kingswear*, B. G. W. Burr.

First published and printed in 1996
reprinted in 2000 by
Obelisk Publications, 2 Church Hill, Pinhoe, Exeter, Devon
Designed and typeset by Sally Barber

Dart Country

DART COUNTRY

The estuary of the River Dart from Kingswear upwards is so striking, and the countryside surrounding it so delightful to explore, that it seemed to require a book to itself. Most people think of the South Hams as the area south of Dartmoor which is bounded by the Yealm and the Dart; but there is a bit extra which seems to have jumped the River Dart and given us the deep valleys and high plateaus so typical of the South Hams, all over again behind Kingswear, Scabbacombe and the Daymark Tower. A 500-foot tableland forms the spine of this area, which runs inland to the north, following the course of the river and narrowing as it goes. It loses height as it approaches Stoke Gabriel. Adding to the interest of this unspoilt stretch of country are four villages, two castles, three old churches, a few stately mansions and a scattering of things prehistoric, to say nothing of miles of good walking where traffic is at a minimum.

As this lovely green belt of agricultural land has the river for its companion most of the time, I think the title "Dart Country" must be the right one. I have much enjoyed the research involved in producing it, and saw with delight many things and places I had never seen before. I hope you will, too.

KINGSWEAR

The best place to start an exploration of Dart Country is at the mouth of the river and slowly to work upwards. So let us begin at Kingswear with its wonderful coast and deep valleys. You are almost certain to approach it from the direction of Paignton, and then will have had to fork right soon after passing Churston station. The upward climb from here to Hillhead (540 ft) is a joy for everyone except the driver, for behind you a wonderful panorama of Torbay, Dartmoor and all the intervening country begins to unfold. Never mind, driver, you will see it all on the way home! At Hillhead take the Lower Ferry Road, and almost immediately the long descent down Slapper's Hill to Kingswear begins. But before continuing, pull in for a moment beside the old tollhouse which shows up quite soon on the left. Here a fine view opens up towards the sea, and it is also a good place to pause to consider how the village we are going to see had its roots up here in these 500-foot hills which rise so grandly beside the river, and not down where Kingswear is today.

This wonderful tract of downland – typical South Hams country, although on the wrong side of the river, maybe, runs in a broad ridge from the Channel coast inland in a north-westerly direction. You will find evidence up here of habitation from early times, for there are (1) an Iron Age fort at Noss Camp, (2) the site of a barrow containing a kist known to have existed near Brownstone, (3) a Romano-British homestead on Basely Common and (4) at a lower level just above Broadsands, a dolmen or chambered tomb.

The prefix "King" immediately challenges the imagination, for besides Kingswear there is the farm of Kingston close by. These names suggest that in the distant past some long-forgotten king owned land here and had a "ware" or lookout place on the coast where watch and ward were kept for enemy shipping. Would that there were documentary evidence for this, but there is the evidence provided by the existence of several ancient farmsteads. The Saxon origin of these is proved at Woodhuish and Coleton, which were Domesday manors. Boohay, too, which is synonymous for the old manor of Levericstone, is mentioned in the mediaeval Cartulary of Torre Abbey. These farms all indicate more dwellings on the manors then than now, and it is most probable that the population lived up in the hills in safety from attack from the sea. Exactly the same thing happened across the river, where the inhabitants lived high above the river at Norton.

An unbroken line of farming folk will therefore have lived and worked in the Kingswear hills, going right back to the times of prehistory. Then, perhaps just before the time of the Norman Conquest, some courageous souls cautiously descended from their hills to live by the river, where they fished and bartered what goods they had. All unknowing, they set in motion that never-ceasing maritime trade for which the ports of Dartmouth and Kingswear were eventually to become famous.

So with these thoughts in mind do up your boot laces, mount that bike or slip in your clutch, as the case may be, and make your way down to the River Dart. The approach road continues down a narrow valley, and soon you will pass Croftland Farm on the right and next a cemetery on the left. On the corner a oneway traffic system takes over and the road turns sharp left. Try your hand here at a few sinuous bends and you will find yourself in Lower Contour Road which is the way to the Lower Ferry. Higher Contour Road, which is on the left, will take you towards the castle and the Devon (South) Coast Path if you happen to be walking or going to the residential part of the village. There is ample parking space on the left of Lower Contour Road, and it's best to get rid of your vehicle here, otherwise you will get swept into the Lower Ferry queue; so your first view of the River Dart may well be from that. If you do get trapped in this way there is still a way out if you drive right down to the railway station and then under the arch. This will lead, not to a watery grave as might be imagined, but to another car park. Everyone should understand, before exploring Kingswear, that it is a village and not a town. It has a population of around 1,500, and it can soon be sensed, as one goes among those fortunate folk who live here, that they belong to that closely knit community which betokens village life.

Be that as it may, neither Kingswear nor Dartmouth would have sprung into existence without their famous river. So all else must bow to the fact that it is the splendid river Dart, beyond all praise in its beauty, which dominates the scene. The towering hills which rise so dramatically on either side may captivate the eye – but only for a moment – then back your gaze will come, like the needle of a compass, to the river, fascinated by the ceaseless activity which goes on there. First there are the two ferries forever plying from the one shore to the other, and then the constant movement of boats of all shapes and sizes. Close by there is always activity at the yacht marina, whilst the occasional puff of white smoke shows where the terminus of the steam train lurks. All these things, and more besides, go to the making of one of the most spectacular river mouths in the south-west.

Dartmouth has, of course, been a thriving port for centuries, but it must not be forgotten that its visual charm depends very much on the splendid line of wooded hills which grace the opposite side of the river. The Victorian villas, too, which cling so precariously to

4

the precipitous hillside, are fine and imposing of their class. They have stood up to well over a century of battering from every wind that blows and look none the worse for it. Kingswear, of course, is more fortunately situated than Dartmouth, for it faces south, stealing all the winter sunshine, when the town across the river is in the shadow of its own hills. Those who bask in this welcome sunshine are also blessed in that they can make a quicker getaway to surrounding towns, for they have no bother with the ferry crossing as do their Dartmouth neighbours, unless they face the long drive round Totnes.

Yet the very life-blood of Kingswear depends on this ferry, for without it the village would have had no reason for existence. Before the days of power-driven boats the ferry would have had to depend on a strong pair of arms or a sail to get across, but as early as 1857 a regular ferry service must have operated, for at the Plume of Feathers a horsedrawn bus awaited passengers who were going to Torquay station to pick up the trains. The advent of the internal combustion engine was soon to herald the arrival of a floating platform, ingeniously attached to a small boat with an outboard engine. This shoved the platform over the river and back swiftly, safely and efficiently. After quite a century of ceaseless activity this apparently primitive method of getting the ferry across has not been improved upon. The Higher Ferry with its sophisticated paddlesteamer was a later arrival. The popularity of the Kingswear ferry was never dreamt of in the early days, and no one could have foreseen the great summer queues of traffic which stretch back a quarter of a mile and more up the hill from the Lower Ferry. This daily phenomenon doubtless brings much casual trade to adjacent shops which line the way, and it is a common thing to see the frustrated occupants of stationary cars leap out of their vehicles to do some hasty shopping whilst still keeping their place in the queue.

Now very few of these people ever think of parking their cars to have a walk around Kingswear itself, but press on all too soon. I can assure them, however, that the high hills on this side of the river are well worth exploring, for they provide a galaxy of riverside views at various levels. The most obvious place to begin a tour of Kingswear is at the ferry slipway. Here there is a shop or two, and it is somehow quite amusing just to wait

a while in the sunshine to see the next ferry come in with its passengers and cars. This will be succeeded by the smiles of joy on the faces of the fortunate drivers who now manage to sweep onto the ferry after waiting in the queue for half an hour – or did I hear you say an hour? If you explore under the archway, you will find yourself in an enclosed, old-world courtyard which boasts one or two fine old sandstone arches. Here you will find another slipway and the Yacht Club. At the far end is Kittery Court, a charmingly situated house right down on the river. This was formerly the home of Brigadier Hine-Haycock, who did so much to preserve the beauty of this coastline for all time.

But this is a cul de sac and as far as you can go in this direction. In the opposite direction stands the former Royal Dart Hotel, which forms one building with the railway station. Until the closure of the line the hotel was always the property of the Great Western Railway; now it is privately owned. The hotel, station and pontoon all form one complex of buildings. The hotel is one of Devon's unusual sights, for it is not often that one sees a hotel whose foundations appear from the river to be in the water. In rough weather the estuary can be very turbulent, and it is a fine sight to see waves lashing the stalwart basement of the building. But they have been doing it since 1864 and seem to have left but little impression. For one thing the hotel was designed in a very solid Italianate style. Facing the river is a fine and spacious saloon which opens out onto a flamboyantly curved iron balcony; its original roof, fenestration and supporting pillars are still intact. The view from the balcony, as might be expected, is quite fascinating, and on a summer's day one can sit there for hours and never grow weary of the prospect of the busy river and the constant movement of the boats upon it. The Royal Dart is no longer a hotel, for though the ground floor is still devoted to catering, the upper floors have been made into flats. The building has certainly seen some changes, not least of which was during the last war when it became the HQ for Coastal Forces and was known as HMS *Cicala*.

Attractive as the river frontage may be, it is the street façade with its rounded windows, so admirably set off by a totally unnecessary clock tower, which is so pleasing. Such whimsicality points to no less a person than Isambard Kingdom Brunel, the great engineer, who fathered the branch line of the railway of which this was the terminus. Although he had died in 1859 it seems probable that all plans for the new line and its attendant buildings would be on his drawing board and were faithfully carried out by R. P. Brereton, his able assistant. There is a distinct resemblance between this little clock tower and the Longpark Pottery tower at Torquay which was meant to be a part of the ill-fated atmospheric railway. Brunel's new home at Watcombe Park was being constructed at about the same time, so it seems that he took a more than usual interest in the branch line which ran so close to it. At Kingswear he seems to have finished with a decided flourish.

The survival of the old covered station is a thing to be proud of, for the advent of the railway simply made Kingswear. A plaque on the station records: "This plaque was unveiled by Sir John Seale May 30th 1989 to commemorate the 125th anniversary of the arrival of the railway at Kingswear". Sir John is a great nephew to Charles Seale, first Chairman of Torbay and Dartmouth Railway Company. The plaque was cast by two students of Paignton College.

The covered passage-way was another interesting thing in the station complex, for it led straight to a pontoon where trains were met by the good steamship *Mew*, known affectionately to generations of Dartmouth people as "Puss-puss". In her good care passengers were swiftly whisked across the river to the never-never station into which a train was never seen to arrive. Apart from a signal box and one or two other attributes Dartmouth station had all the other fittings of a Great Western station – particularly the booking office, paintwork and seats. The buildings have now been put to other uses, but the station still functions as a landing-stage for

railway passengers. Paignton became the terminus, however, when the line was axed under Beeching. In 1972 a newly formed Dart Valley Railway Co. reopened the Paignton–Kingswear section as a holidaymakers' steam-train line. It is staffed by full-time volunteers and trains are pulled by locomotive 4555.

In the good old days there was a late Saturday afternoon train to Paddington known as the "Honeymoon Express". The story is told how one Saturday afternoon the station-master was confronted by a despairing bridegroom who had just failed to jump aboard the train in time, whilst the bride went off with the best man who had failed to jump off! But all ended well – a taxi was to hand which got the perspiring bridegroom to Newton Abbot before the train!

Above the station a footbridge crosses the line, leading to Darthaven Marina which was constructed in 1978; it is one of the largest in the district and can accommodate over 230 vessels. An administration block was added in 1993, which contains houses for staff, chandlery, workshops, showers etc. From here a riverside path goes towards the Higher Ferry and the site of Britannia Halt, which was once the station for the Royal Naval College just across the water. The road from here leads back to Hillhead, but apart from an active shipyard a quarter of a mile on there is nothing more to be seen at this end of Kingswear. So it is now time to return to the village itself and see all it has to offer. The most prominent building, as one views the hillside from the river, is the church. So it may be a good thing to explore this first and then to work along Castle Road, which takes one out towards the mouth of the river and the two castles; but on the way it will be worth our while to pause to admire some of the fine houses which nestle so happily on the well-wooded hillside.

THE PARISH CHURCH OF ST THOMAS OF CANTERBURY

The Parish Church is a small but pleasing building whose squat tower and twin gables show up prominently from the river. It is situated on the south side of the precipitous hill on which the village stands, and it is interesting to note that an old map of c.1540 shows a spire surmounting the tower. The dedication to St Thomas of Canterbury is thought to be because this was a place whence pilgrims set out who were making for the shrine of St Thomas à Becket in Canterbury Cathedral. Of all the pilgrim routes thither this was said to be the longest. A great wave of devotion for this saint sprang up after his murder in 1170, and it is quite feasible that pilgrims from the Continent landed here, and after a service in St Thomas's church, set out upon their arduous journey. A Norman, or even a Saxon chapel may have existed here prior to 1170, but there is no documentation for it, neither is its dedication known.

It seems reasonable to suppose that the church was built, or maybe only enlarged, about this time and lasted until 1847, when it must have been in bad condition for it was demolished all but the tower. A local architect, E. Appleton, designed the new church and built it on the old foundations. Indeed its appearance on eighteenth century prints is exactly the same as now. There are also old interments in the aisles which appear in situ. Quite a few things survive from the old church, however, including the fourteenth century octagonal font.

You never know, in a Devon church, what surprises may await you even in the humblest of buildings. There are two here, for instance. First there is a splendid array of carved wooden angels supporting the bases of the roof beams. There are ten on each side in the nave and nine a side in the south aisle, making a total of no less than thirty-eight. They probably date from the fifteenth century, and thanks to the architect's love of things mediaeval were considered too good to discard in the 1847 rebuilding. The angels are varied in design, and larger than might have been expected. Choose a bright day for your visit and take your binoculars with you, for being almost black in colour, they are hard to see. How magnificent they would look if one day their fifteenth century style of colouring were restored.

A second surprise awaits behind the choir stalls: it is the stone lid of what must have been an elaborate altar tomb. Round the edges, in Norman French, is the inscription, "You who pray for Philip shall have 30 days of pardon as a reward". So who was this Philip that he was given so fine a tomb? The Rev B. G. W. Burr in his booklet on the church points out that there was a Brother Philip Fitzurse who was Parish Priest of Arlington in North Devon in 1258. Now one of the knights who murdered St Thomas à Becket was Richard Fitzurse. He founded one or two churches in part expiation of his crime; Kingswear could have been one. Philip, in the next century, could have been a descendant of Richard and appointed to Kingswear because the gift of the living remained in the Fitzurse family. Philip Fitzurse, a "monk of Kingswear" is mentioned in the mid-thirteenth century (*Devon Feet of Fines*) and again in a local law court. So the fact that he was a descendant of the founder of the church could explain his elaborate tomb cover. An ancient tomb is said to have been removed when the organ was built, and it was relegated to the churchyard. But the Rev. Burr rescued it, and it is there in the south aisle for you to see.

Other relics of the older church are a bell, dated 1680, and a fine silver ciborium made from an older chalice and paten in 1640. The building of 1847 is light and spacious. It contains much good woodwork, especially in the pulpit, tastefully carved bench ends and choirstalls. The clock in the tower marks Queen Victoria's sixtieth anniversary.

The status of the church was a Chapel of Ease to St Mary's, Brixham, but in 1837 it achieved parochial status. Until 1539 it belonged to and was served by Totnes Priory.

Visitors should not omit reading the exceedingly moving citation on the north wall which commemorates the gallant death of Colonel Herbert Jones VC, OBE (locally known as "H"), who gave his life in the Falklands War in 1982, whilst commanding the 2nd Battalion The Parachute Regiment. "H" was a native of Kingswear and was brought up at The Grange, a house high in the hills above the Castle. The framed citation begins as follows:

IN THANKFUL MEMORY

OF THOSE OF THIS PARISH

WHO GAVE THEIR LIVES IN WAR

FALKLANDS 1982

HERBERT JONES, VC, OBE

It then goes on to relate how on 28th May, 1982, Lt Col. Jones was commanding the 2nd Battalion The Parachute Regiment on operations in the Falkland Islands. The Battalion was ordered to attack enemy divisions on and around the settlement of Darwin and Goose Green. The enemy were found to occupy at least eleven trenches and were well dug in. After an hour's fighting during which casualties were sustained Colonel Jones took a reconnaissance party forward, but to little avail. He eventually decided that desperate measures were needed to overcome the enemy position. It seemed to him a moment for personal leadership. Seizing a sub-machine-gun, and with complete disregard for his own safety, he charged the nearest enemy position. As he advanced up a short slope he was hit and seen to fall, but he immediately picked himself up and, with supreme courage, charged the enemy once again. He was thus open to fire from all directions and fell dying only a few feet from the enemy trench. This devastating display of courage completely undermined the enemy's morale and they soon surrendered to a company of the Battalion. As a direct result Darwin and Goose Green were quickly liberated, the inhabitants quite unharmed, and some 1,200 of the enemy surrendered. This achievement of the 2nd Battalion set the tone for the subsequent land victory on the

Falklands, the enemy never doubting the superiority of the British troops and their own ultimate defeat.

"H's" gallant action was at the time an inspiration to all about him and smacks of the great deeds of chivalry and daring which are a part of our history.

KINGSWEAR CASTLE

A castle by the sea is surely the answer to all one's romantic yearnings, but when in addition it is all but hidden by thick woods of maritime firs and surrounded by towering hills, then indeed we are in for something that might have come straight from one of Hans Andersen's fairy tales. Here in South Devon, at the mouth of the Dart, we have just this in Kingswear Castle – one of the least known and least visited of all the castles in Britain. If you decide to seek it out my advice to you is to do it on foot if possible and not by sea, for the approach by land is much more charming, and by the time you get there you will have walked along beautiful quiet roads, high up above the river, which allow many a peep of the sea beyond. So set out from the church and proceed along Castle Road. You will see how the lovely scenery forms an excellent appetiser for what you are going to visit. Eventually a pair of iron gates, hung on stalwart gateposts, will appear on the right. From here a steep drive takes the visitor, after about a quarter of a mile, down to the castle, which suddenly comes into sight far below. The first thing that strikes people is its smallness – a mere pocket-sized castle, surely; the second thing is that it seems almost in the sea. Indeed on stormy days waves do break right over it, the water falling eventually on the threshold of the front door.

The castle, though small, is full of interest; it is built of the local stone which, just here, is grey in colour. This is relieved by red sandstone, which is liberally used in the dressings of the doors, windows and corbel table. For all its smallness Kingswear is a real castle with turrets, battlements and machicolations whence you may pour down all kinds of horrors on unwanted callers. These features, together with the main doorway, slit windows and corbel table, all suggest a mid-fourteenth century date. Yet the castle is said to date only from 1501 when King Henry VII decided to defend the approach to his port of Dartmouth against the French. He spent £68.19s.0½d in doing so! But if we accept a fourteenth century date for the castle, then this outlay must have been spent entirely on the insertion of several business-like gunports to an already existing building. And indeed why should it not have been? So the much strengthened building, together with Dartmouth Castle directly opposite, then commanded this important harbour. The

building of such blockhouses in pairs was not uncommon and may be seen again at Fowey. It is interesting to record that at the beginning of the sixteenth century these two castles were considered the most up-to-date on our coasts, the reason being that they had splayed gunports. Hitherto guns in castles were only able to fire straight ahead, whereas with the newly adopted splayed gunports they were able to cover a wider range, for the guns could be swung round. Kingswear had gunports on three sides, and on each of its three floors. On the first and second floors there were extra gunports at about four feet from the floor – these guns being mounted on platforms. The roof was also used, so it can be understood how this little castle was a veritable hornets' nest.

Its value as an active battery was short-lived, nevertheless, for by mid-century the range of guns had been greatly increased. So as soon as the Dartmouth guns could command the river from bank to bank Kingswear Castle became obsolete and therefore redundant. In 1583, however, Sir John Gilbert recommended "4 pieces of ordnance royal", saying that they should be of brass, "for the breath of the sea will consume quickly iron ordnance". In the seventeenth century, at the outbreak of the Civil War, Dartmouth declared for Parliament, but it was taken by Prince Maurice in 1643. Then in 1646 it was taken by Fairfax, but Kingswear Castle seems never to have been in Royalist hands, though the Redoubt on the top of the hill certainly was. In 1642 there is mention of making "4 deal dores for Kingswear Castle 4s 0d." This suggests that the building was run down at the start of the Civil War and was then being repaired. There was a fire there at this period, and whether this was intentional on the part of the Parliamentarians is not known. With the hill so close behind it could certainly never have been defended from a land attack. This may be why Col. Cary went to the trouble of making the Redoubt.

After the Restoration in 1660 the Crown took over the upkeep of both castles from the Corporation of Dartmouth. Fears of a Dutch invasion prompted hasty repairs. Large

cannons are reported to have been on the roof at Kingswear at this time. As 160 guns are mentioned at the port of Dartmouth, a large proportion of them would have been at Kingswear. At the coming of peace, however, the castle would become neglected again and perhaps even deserted. A report in 1717 by one of His Majesty's "Ingeniers" states that there were four guns at Kingswear on top, all mounted on unserviceable carriages, and the tower itself "useless and irreparable". After this period there would be yet another period of neglect until the castle was gradually abandoned altogether. Two of its cannons, known as "sakers", were apparently thrown into the sea, where they still lie – waiting to be rescued along with the chain which once stretched across the river. Judging from water-colours and sketches of the period, many of which survive, the castle was falling gently into decay with the parapet collapsing. This unhappy epoch must have lasted for well over a century, and had the building not been rescued in 1855 by Charles Hayne Seale Hayne we should have had another sad, ruined castle to join nearby Berry Pomeroy.

Having traced the history of the castle to modern times, let us explore the building itself and try to imagine how it was equipped in time of war. In the first place there is only one door to enter by, and this is only 2 ft 6 in wide; so only in single file may you enter here. But pause to admire the lovely warm, red sandstone of which the pointed arch is composed; then step carefully down the steep steps into the gunroom. If you have closed the door behind you, and the shutters of the gunports happen to be closed, the room is pretty well in darkness, for there are no windows. Notice how the gunports are splayed, for it was on this then novel feature that the strength of the little castle depended. There is a built-up fireplace in the back wall and on the right the one and only stair turret. At the foot of the stair a vaulted passage on the right leads to a small tower which was added in 1855 by the architect Lidstone. This is a most delightful folly which, from the river, looks most convincing. The tower is round, yet the room within is pentagonal, with groined vaulting and an excellent replica of a sixteenth century fireplace. Here the arms of the Seale and Hayne families are displayed. The windows, which look out in two directions, give attractive views of the harbour and out to sea. In the dimness of the passage and in this room there are mysterious doors and staircases which throw out dark hints of oubliettes and gruesome secrets. The tower room is the only room in the building where there is a feeling of charm and intimacy – all the rest still retain their military starkness.

Before ascending to the first floor, notice the fine floor which the Landmark Trust have inserted, thus restoring the floor to its old level. The gunports on the first floor are differently distributed to the those on the ground floor – one on the left-hand side, four in the centre and three on the right. In the centre ones, athwart the sills, there remain blocks of wood with pivot holes on which the guns could be swung. There are also two extra gunports at about four feet from the floor, much higher than the rest. Their apertures have crude shoulder arches. The guns themselves must have been mounted on platforms.

Most interesting of all is a rounded window on the left-hand wall beneath which is a garde-robe with wooden seat still intact. It is placed in a recess in the thickness of the wall. Seale Hayne, we are told, disguised this as a wine cellar.

The second floor, now furnished as a lounge-kitchen, was the third gunroom, with three gunports in front, two on the right and two on the left. The castle abounds in narrow slit windows, mostly facing to the rear with its hilly approach. Some in the (by then) obsolete style are circular at the bottom to accommodate a hand gun, which could only fire straight ahead. Best of all is the one in the modern bathroom which graces the turret. Here you may lie in your bath and pot at the enemy on the hill behind or, if you're lucky, get a rabbit for your pot. The delightful turret is original, but the crenellation on the roof is part of the 1855 restoration. The old roof level was lower than at present and guns were also mounted here. There are also two socket holes in the rear wall, which were the supports for a covered platform from which an enemy on the hill could be discomfited.

So by and large this castle was certainly not lacking in defences, in addition to its considerable attacking potential where enemy shipping was concerned. If required, it could have housed as many as twenty-five or thirty guns. These had intriguing names, too, for there were "sakers", "murderers" and "serpyntynes".

It is delightful to see how the little building has been recently put into such good shape by the Landmark Trust, with heating and all mod. cons. – the purpose being that you, too, can go and stay there if you wish for as long a holiday as you like. You have only to contact the Trust. So the building appears to be in good hands for the foreseeable future. There would, of course, by this time have been not one stone upon another had it not been for the energy and determination of one man, who snatched it from the ruin which threatened it in 1855. This was Charles Hayne Seale Hayne (1833–1903). Born Charles Hayne Seale, he was the son of Sir John Seale, Bart, for many years MP for Dartmouth. He inherited,whilst still a youth, a large fortune from his great-uncle, providing that he took the surname of Hayne, which he did. He was called to the Bar but never practised. Instead he became a politician and was MP for Ashburton for many years. He was also a Privy Councillor. Though residing at Pitt House, Chudleigh, during the winter, he spent his summers at Kingswear Castle. It was largely through his efforts that the railway reached Kingswear in 1864. He left money for the founding of an Agricultural College outside Newton Abbot which bears his name. So it was this public figure who, as a young man of 22, bought Kingswear Castle and rescued it from ruin with all the ardour of youth. He was ably assisted in his project by Thomas Lidstone, a local architect of experience who had built Waddeton Court and rebuilt the chapel there and several other houses. He not only made the castle habitable but did much structural work, restoring the parapet and building the intriguing tower west of the main block, which he joined to the castle by a short passage. All this appears so mediaeval that it deceives most people.

On the death of Charles a purchase was made by the Rev. Harold Burton. In the mid-twenties he was succeeded by Major L. Wright, TD. Then came the Second World War, when the castle was commandeered and occupied by Marines. They built the concrete blockhouse, which still stands just as it was built in 1940. After the war the castle stood empty until 1957, when it was bought by Sir Frederick Bennett – MP for Torbay. He did the repairs then necessary and made the building habitable once more. When he retired in 1987 a purchase was made by the Landmark Trust, who cannot be praised too much for the first-rate work they have carried out. This was finally completed in 1990.

GOMEROCK CASTLE

This is the second and older of Kingswear's two castles. It is today a forgotten and deserted ruin, situated immediately opposite Dartmouth Castle, and romantically perched above the rock which gives it its name. It stands some 150 feet above the river and so was in an ideal spot to withstand attacks from the marauders who harried the coasts so much in the Middle Ages. But from the moment that firearms, and later cannons, were introduced, then Gomerock became useless, for it was far too high above the river to aim at ships broadside on. Dartmouth and Kingswear Castles were built lower down and only a few feet above the waterline at high tide. So Gomerock was abandoned as a castle; yet for years it was to maintain an important part in the defence of the river, for it was from here that the famous chain was stretched across to Dartmouth Castle, blocking the entry to the river. Gomerock Castle is clearly marked on the 1540 map of the estuary where it is shown to be a castellated tower with two turrets. It is referred to in 1590 as "the old castelle of Kingswear" – "old" because it had been superseded by Kingswear Castle in 1501. A lease of 1590 shows that it was then owned by Gawen Champernowne. Deeds later than 1656 describe it as "a mansion ruined in the last warres", i.e. the Civil War, when Parliamentarians perhaps blew it up or burnt it, as was the case with Kingswear, thus rendering it useless to the Royalists. And a ruin it has remained. To date this castle is difficult, but it must have been built far earlier than 1495, when plans for Kingswear Castle were first mooted. It is, for instance, hard to believe that there was no defence on this side of the river in Norman times, but whether this was it only a long-overdue excavation will tell.

From a distance nothing can be seen of the old castle today, for thick woodland has encroached upon it. But from the river the Gomerock itself can be examined, and it shows itself as a steep-sided rock with a flat top which thrusts itself out from the surrounding cliffs. Prominent to the eye is a strange platform on top – strange because the perpendicular cliff face at the back of the rock contains numerous man-made holes, apparently joist holes. This suggests that a building once stood here, which could have been some kind of outer defence or the place whence the chain went across. Before the cliff face is a small well, or man-made pool, which still contains water.

Proceeding from here up steep and narrow steps one eventually reaches the castle. Three rectangular buildings now appear. The first has been a bakery, for at its far end is a large hearth in whose back wall is a huge oven. This suggests that there was once a large garrison to provide for. Beyond is a small building at a higher level where we are transported to the present century with a jolt, for affixed to the cliff-face, which does duty as a rear wall, are memorial tablets to no less than seventeen dogs. They all date from the turn of the century – "Kipsie", "Tazzie", "Mini", among fourteen others. Each name is inscribed on a small, square plaque affixed to a large wall tablet, of which there are two.

The third building is the castle itself, which towers above the bakehouse on a rocky mound. Its walls are five feet thick, and its shape is a quadrilateral 43 ft 6 in by 29 ft 8 in. But on the first and second floors the building extends into the irregular cliff-face by a further 5 ft 4 in with an apsidal ending. There are two hearths in the thickness of the walls, one having a circular brick-lined oven. It seems to me that this is by far the most exciting building in Kingswear and no doubt the oldest. A thorough examination of the site is long overdue and might reveal much of an unsuspected nature. The castle is privately owned.

BROOKHILL

Before we leave Kingswear to explore the surrounding coast and country, mention must be made of some of the delightful houses and their well-established gardens which grace the wooded hillside. Those close to the water have their own jetties, but even those high up on the hill have contrived to make their own private steps which lead eventually down to some attractive cove or other where boats can make a landing. Above Kettle Cove, for instance, stands Brookhill, one of the earlier houses. It was built in the early nineteenth century by Arthur Howe Holdsworth, hereditary Governor of Dartmouth Castle and MP for that town. The first house was built in 1820 and collapsed into the sea. The present house, with glorious views of the river and surrounding hills, was built much higher up. During the last war it became the headquarters of the Free French Navy. It was later a Country Club and now is divided into several very desirable flats. The interesting panelling and plasterwork remaining ably demonstrate that this was once a well-appointed mansion. A terraced garden of great charm leads by way of many flights of steps down to Kettle Cove.

KINGSWEAR COURT AND SILVER COVE

Most of the houses on the hill date from the middle of the nineteenth century, but a few only from the turn of the century. One of these is Kingswear Court which stands high above the Castle. Its grounds, like Brookhill's, extend far down the cliff to the sea itself and are a maze of steps, terraces and secluded paths. At sea level a gate leads to Silver Cove and some interesting remains. Just after the First World War, Sir Thomas Lennard, the owner of Kingswear Court, constructed a swimming pool which was filled by the sea at each high tide. Its upper end extended into a cave within the cliff. When war broke out again in 1939 Silver Cove suddenly leapt into importance as a base for launching torpedoes. A concrete platform was constructed over the pool and this still exists; so do a concrete storehouse and a slipway where the torpedoes were launched. This occupies all the tiny beach of the cove. No doubt everything was top secret at the time, and the good folk living around never knew how well protected they were.

Today the swimming pool is still mostly covered by the concrete platform, but from its top end it is possible to gaze down into the swirling waters of the sea as they wash into the cave below. Perhaps most remarkable of all is the folly – a round granite battlemented tower, standing about 30 feet in height. It contains nothing but a spiral stair which leads into space, for the first floor has disintegrated. An inscribed stone at the base of the tower states, "Lady Lennard 9.9.19". She is also commemorated in the church by a tablet.

IN THE KINGSWEAR HILLS

From the railway station Kingswear looks a most unpromising place for walking, but the reverse is really the case. However, to get going one has to get up into the hills above the river. You will not go far wrong if you begin all your walks from the church and climb upwards to Castle Road. Your map will show how some quite lengthy circular tours can be done, beginning by way of the Devon (South) Coast Path. This begins at Castle Mill Cove and then leads past Newfoundland Cove, Kelly's Cove, Pudcombe Cove, Scabbacombe Cove, Long Sands and Man Sands and eventually takes you right out of Dart Country towards St Mary's Bay and Berry Head. If you wish to explore inland, a little past Newfoundland Cove you will come to some old concrete gun emplacements. Here a lane on the left leads to the summit of the 500-foot plateau, passing beside the Daymark Tower. Here are Coleton Fishacre (where the house and garden are open to the public), Kingston, Boohay, Brownstone and Nethway. A left turn before reaching Boohay leads back to Kingswear past Fountain Violet Farm, whence there are magnificent views of the river, and next past the Redoubt – an earthwork, constructed in the Civil War, which was particularly strong because the banks had stone facings. It was held by Colonel Cary for the Royalists in 1646; he surrendered it, however, to Fairfax the day after the latter took Dartmouth.

The views on the summit of the plateau are extensive, with the English Channel to the south, Start Bay to the south-west, and on the skyline behind you the good old hills of Dartmoor. The National Trust owns considerable tracts of woodland along the coast, and they also own a carpark near the Daymark Tower which is a useful spot at which to leave your car when using this as a starting point for a walk. Allow at least two full days to discover all the secrets of the coastline – the pleasures of the secluded beaches, the horrors of Rock Lane and the breathtaking staircase above Castle Mill Cove. At the top of this, beside the road, stands a plaque set in granite which commemorates Lt Col. H. Jones, who lived nearby at The Grange, which you will pass on the way to Brownstone via Rock Lane. His exploits and valiant death have already been mentioned. This section of Warren Woods is dedicated to his memory.

THE DAYMARK TOWER

Half a mile inland, and to the north of Inner Froward Point, stands the Daymark Tower which was built in 1864. It has braved the elements on a lonely and deserted hilltop for over 130 years. As the entrance to Dartmouth harbour is so narrow it is hard to see from the Channel; so this daymarker was built as an aid to navigation by Dartmouth Harbour Commissioners. In 1870 it was taken over by Trinity House for 1,000 years at a rent of 1s. per annum. It is a weird and solitary object to come across on a foggy day, when its gaunt form looms up suddenly out of the mist. It is octagonal in shape with slender arched openings on each of its eight sides. As a result, from whichever side you view it you can always see right through it.

The interior resembles a huge chimney and is 80ft. in height. It stands in the middle of a field (private), but on the west side is a stile and a short path which gives access to it. A notice reminds that although seeming so aloof and silent, the tower is actually in daily use by shipping, for on approaching the coast it appears on the horizon before the hills on which it stands, thus providing a precise bearing for ships entering the River Dart.

COLETON FISHACRE

To reach the plateau on which Coleton Fishacre and the Daymark Tower stand, approach Kingswear as before via Hillhead, but soon after the descent of Slapper's Hill begins there appears on the left the old tollhouse, with a deserted school behind, where we paused before. This time take the left fork, bearing in mind that this is the old road from Kingswear which climbed out of the village by way of the precipitous Wood Lane. This is the way that in the Middle Ages the pilgrims took when they began their long trek to the shrine of St Thomas in Canterbury Cathedral. So by the time they got to where you are now they would have experienced their first taste of what Devon hills can be like and be feeling rather puffed. So, if I were you I should just pull in to let them go by!

In a quarter of a mile you will pass Nethway on your left and Boohay on the right, after which the road makes for Coleton Fishacre whose entrance appears at the top of a hill. The house is not old but its history is interesting: it was built in or about 1924 at the instigation of Rupert D'Oyly Carte, son of Richard D'Oyly Carte, the business partner of Gilbert and Sullivan. The sheltered valley below the old farm of the Fishaker family provided an ideal site for a new house and the opportunity of creating an outstanding garden. Oswald Milne, of the firm of Lutyens, was the architect for the house and the formal garden. The latter was developed by Lady Dorothy D'Oyly Carte and she took advantage of the sheltered combe in which it lay and of the stream which flows down to the sea. There is a superb collection of trees of many different species and flowering shrubs in profusion. The slope leads down to Pudcombe Cove. The garden was acquired by the National Trust in 1983.

The Fisaker family were active in the thirteenth and fourteenth centuries, and from them the place took its name. Torre Abbey Cartulary contains a charter of 1331 wherein Ives de ffisthacre rented three ferlings of land in Ludewycheton, the old name for the manor of Boohay, which his forbears had held. The various spellings of the name Fishacre are quite bewildering!

THE CONNECTION OF TORRE ABBEY WITH KINGSWEAR

This may be a good place to digress to explain the connection of Torre Abbey with Kingswear, which was a long one. In the Exchequer Cartulary there are twelve charters under the heading of "Kyngeswere". The most important of these is the first, whereby Walter de Vasci gives all his land at Kyngeswere to the Canons of Torre, excepting that part which belongs to the Prior of Totnes. You can read elsewhere of the de Vasci family and their ownership of Kingswear. It seems that the family gave half their land to Totnes Priory, whilst at a later date the rest went to Torre Abbey. There is also mention of "Kitetorra", which as Kittery was to become the hub of the village. These charters date mostly from the twelfth or early thirteenth century. A good deal of the Abbey property lay up in the hills, round the present farm of Boohay. There is evidence of an early settlement here called "Lydewichestone" or "Lethewiston", and this was a mediaeval manor. Here were three ferlings (about seventy-five acres) which were given to the Abbey by the Fizaker family, and also three acres at Horestone – a part of the long-forgotten tenement of Watersipe. Michael, who owned the last-mentioned land, says that his brother, William, died whilst defending it. This chance reference to a skirmish of the thirteenth century makes interesting reading; would that we knew more about it. Two fields near Nethway marked on an old map as Little and Lower Orestone may very well be the land mentioned.

The Abbey was dissolved in 1539, and by this time Kingswear had become a separate manor, existing side by side with "Bowhaye alias Lethwiston". At this time the lord of Totnes evidently exacted toll on all fish landed at Kingswear, but in the Dublin Cartulary it is recorded that twenty-four of the Abbot of Torre's men living at Kingswear were exempted from this toll. Grazing rights at "Wodehiwis and Liddewigetune" are also mentioned in a thirteenth century charter. So it will be seen from all this that from, say, 1200 to 1539 Torre Abbey wielded great power over the population on this side of the river.

NETHWAY

Probably the most interesting old house in the neighbourhood is Nethway, whose drive is immediately opposite Boohay. It is a large house of three storeys and a half basement, consisting of seven by five bays. It would at one time present its grey-brick construction to the world, but it is now stuccoed on two sides. Its rather plain exterior is forgotten on entering, for the house is both gracious and well-proportioned. There is much in the way of panelling and decorated ceilings. The main staircase is wide with a handsome balustrade, whilst the landings are spacious. Everywhere there is an abundance of light, especially in those rooms which have windows on either side

The servants' staircase is remarkable for having a newel post which comes right up from the cellar through four storeys. It was once a ship's mast. John Fownes, who built the house in 1699, made a fortune by trading with the West Indies; so it is tempting to think that the mast may have come from one of his ships and found safe anchorage here. The half cellars have many windows – all of which are now blocked. This shows how banks have at some time been constructed round the house. There is a long vaulted passage which is separated from the rest of the cellar by a thick wall and appears mediaeval in construction. It may have been a damp course. An older house once stood here; and this may be the only remaining part of it. There is also an interesting water-tank which is slate-lined and fed by a spring in the hillside. This must be the old water supply of the house.

A plaque in the hall records that Charles II spent a night at Nethway in 1671, but that must have been in the former house. An exterior wall tablet states, "The within house was built by John Fownes Anno Domini 1699". In fact it was a certain John Hody who began to build the house, but sold to Fownes before completion. It is refreshing to see so fine a house still lived in by a family. It is, of course, private and not open to the public.

NOSS CAMP

Up in the hills, a few degrees south of west from Hillhead Farm, and at a distance of three quarters of a mile, stands Noss Camp, also known as Greenway Camp or Hillhead Camp. Situated at a height of over 300 feet, it stands astride the spur of a hill which divides the headwaters of two streams which quickly reach Noss Creek. Defences on the lower side consist of a single bank and a deep, broad ditch. On the higher side are two lines of defences, now in scrub, yet well preserved. A third line crosses the spur to the north and is incorporated into a hedge bank. The entrances are considered to be in the centre of the main enclosure, but are obscured by a later field bank and lynchets. No excavation has ever taken place, but the fort is considered to be prehistoric and of the Iron Age. Mediaeval finds made in 1949 are in Torquay Museum. The fort is situated on land belonging to Hillhead Farm.

CHURSTON FERRERS

This is the only part of Dart Country which contains a thickly populated urban area; for at its northern tip a quiet rural countryside suddenly ends with a bump at Churston station. After this the remaining half mile of the parish is a continuation of a very pleasant built-up area which began at Goodrington, on the outskirts of Paignton. Churston Ferrers has water on two sides – Torbay, at Broadsands and Elberry Cove, and the River Dart from Waddeton downwards, to the west. The sandy stretch of Broadsands is a wonderful family beach with safe bathing. On the way down the road takes you under Brunel's splendid railway viaduct of nine arches. If you want things a bit quieter than at Broadsands, then walk round to Elberry Cove, so picturesquely set with its background of woodland. The beach here is stony, and beware of bathing from the rocks where there is deep water.

The beaches soon give way to green fields, and the rest of the parish, apart from the two villages of Churston Ferrers and Galmpton, is agricultural at the present time. The church, manor house and dignified farmhouse stand in refreshing rural isolation; they are a quarter of a mile from the village, which consists of nineteenth century estate-built houses and one shop. The well-designed schoolhouse of 1864 was advertised in modern times by a house agent as a "character home", complete with the old school bell!

So Churston can offer attractive beaches on Torbay, boating on the Dart at Galmpton Creek and Greenway, and an eighteen-hole golf course near Churston station. There are also two houses of standing at Churston Court and Lupton House; an interesting old church; an old village at Galmpton; and last, but not least, the fine open stretch of Galmpton Warborough with its War Memorial and ruined windmill of red sandstone. So if you're out of breath after seeing all that, I never mentioned where the Weary Ploughman was, did I, Joe? Or was it the White Horse?

CHURSTON STATION

We are apt to take the Kingswear railway line very much for granted these days and quite forget the numerous difficulties which beset Brunel when he planned the line in the

1850s. The railway had reached Torre in 1848, and this was meant to be the terminus. It was to be a decade and more before the needs of Paignton, Brixham and Dartmouth were considered. The railway reached Paignton in 1859, Churston (first called Brixham Road) in 1861 and Kingswear in 1864. From Paignton onwards the last section of the line involved various difficulties. First came the marshes at Goodrington; then the long viaduct at Broadsands and a short one before it; Churston station and its attendant hotel; a considerable tunnel at Greenway; another viaduct at Maypool; marshes beside the river; and finally a bridge over the creek just outside Kingswear station. An expensive line, for certain. Meanwhile there had been much bickering over the direction of the final section of the line, Dartmouth people naturally pressing for a terminus there, with a bridge over the Dart. Eventually (and for certain regretfully) the line was taken to Kingswear as its terminus.

It is of Churston station, however, of which I wish to write in particular, for it was a typical railway junction of the period, quite comfortless, and at that time in the middle of nowhere. Imagine being dumped down at Churston in 1861 on a black night in winter when an easterly gale was blowing and the rain coming down in buckets. You had been travelling for hours already, probably from Paddington, and for certain, were perished with cold; and all this to find that the last train to Brixham had left an hour ago! But there was hope! The railway company, with a flash of true inspiration, had built a good solid hotel in the station yard where blessed warmth and comfort could be readily obtained. There, after regaling yourself with what I am sure was excellent fare, you could contemplate with equanimity the prospect of being able only to get to Brixham that night by a horsedrawn cab, or else to stay the night at the hotel and catch the first train down in the morning, which went at 4 a.m. (did I hear you say?) to pick up the fish.

It's there yet, that hotel, very much more in the middle of things now than then. It looks as though it may not have altered one bit since those Victorian times. Its name, strangely enough, is constantly changing and at the moment it is the Weary Ploughman, whilst a nearby companion is the White Horse.

The people of Galmpton, Kingswear and Brixham were fortunate ever to have had a railway so early in the century. It is splendid that the line still functions in the summer months, though regrettable that the short branch to Brixham was never re-opened after Beeching's closure of the Kingswear line. A few of its bridges still stand near Churston Ferrers as a reminder of the former two-mile-long branch line.

THE CHURCH OF ST MARY THE VIRGIN

Churston Church and Court form visually a happy partnership. They are so close to one another that there is only the width of a narrow path between them. It is not hard to surmise, therefore that the church was once the private chapel of the Court. In 1088, however, the tithe was granted to Totnes Priory; in 1136 the church itself. Then in 1480 it became a parish church attached to Brixham. From this date will stem the enlarging of the church in the perpendicular style – in fact the building of today. So a church on the site goes back at least 900 years.

The building consists of nave, aisles, a low western tower and a three-storeyed south porch. It is surprisingly spacious for a church situated, until recently, in a thinly populated rural area. Even today green fields surround it.

The main characteristics of the building are its ample width and lightness. The oldest part is the south-west corner, porch and tower; the blocked doorway at the end of the aisle may well be a relic of the old Norman chapel. All the rest is of the late perpendicular style. The main feature of the exterior is not the tower but the dignified south porch, whose gable rises so strikingly beside the aisle roof. It is much enhanced by the fine cornerstones of sandstone and by a large stoup. Best of all are the remains of what appears to be a lantern cross, whose head is set in the wall above the parvise (porch room) window. It retains a canopied Crucifixion with attendant figures. Joist holes in the wall of the parvise show that there was yet another floor above. The parvise has a fireplace and must have been a solar for the monks of Totnes Priory. In the splay of the parvise window is a quatrefoil opening which overlooks the interior of the church. Such an opening is claimed to be unique in Devon. Note in the porch itself the roundheaded doorways of the late Norman period.

There is no chancel arch and no rood screen, these factors greatly contributing to the

spaciousness of the church. Fragments of the rood screen are worked into the screen which now separates nave and tower. The tall piers are of Beer stone, their capitals curiously wrought with weird monsters – a great bird carrying a horse-shoe, a winged mermaid, two men and eight human faces, to say nothing of serpents! The most easterly capital shows the arms of Yarde, Wadham, Hales, Ferrers, Bampfylde and Bozon. Note how the position of the rood stair shows that the chancel had two bays and the nave only three.

The roofs display a complete set of old bosses of superior design, no two being alike. Some mediaeval glass has been assembled in the easternmost window of the south aisle. Shields of the Champernowne and other local families are displayed. In the east window there is modern glass by James Paterson (1957). It was given by Dame Agatha Christie, the playwright and novelist, who lived at Greenway House nearby.

In the Sanctuary is a fine piscina of Beer stone which has a shelf and is surmounted by a cinquefoiled ogee arch. There is also a squint or hagioscope in the same wall.

The font has an old base on which are the shields of eight distinguished families. The bowl dates only from c.1736, so it cannot be the one in which Sir Humphrey Gilbert was christened, for he was born in about 1539 at Greenway House.

The tower contains interesting bells, the oldest dating from 1440. It was cast by Robert Norton of Exeter. Two others were cast in 1460. All three have Latin inscriptions and are part of a ring of six.

There is an excellent organ by Walker. It was formerly in St Michael's church, Pimlico, Torquay, and was brought here when that church was demolished. Another item rescued from the same church is the reredos in the Lady chapel, which began life at Throwleigh, where it stood behind the high altar. The panels were carved at Oberammergau.

Over the south door is a good example of Queen Anne's coat of arms, dating from 1713. An interesting relic is a sixteenth century iron chest; it has two locks and is said to be of Spanish origin.

A prized possession is a fine Elizabethan chalice and paten lid of 1574. The knob of the paten is decorated with a Tudor rose. There is also a silver alms dish (1710), a silver flagon of the same date and finally a large silver paten. But let would-be burglars please note that these objects are not in residence and give their address as the Bank!

There is an interesting story in Beatrix Cresswell's book on Devonshire parsons: it tells of Peter Grigg, who was vicar here 1638–46, at a time when Prayer Book services were forbidden and clergy using them subject to severe penalties. One Sunday, whilst the vicar was using the Prayer Book service, a Cromwellian soldier appeared. Holding a pistol to the vicar's head he ordered him to stop. But the vicar calmly finished the prayer, after which he said, "I have done my duty as a Minister, now you can do yours as a soldier". According to Beatrix Cresswell the abashed soldier slunk away, but another version has it that the vicar was arrested and marched away; I wonder which is true? So by and large the story of the church here is of more than usual interest.

CHURSTON COURT

After visiting the church the next thing on the agenda is to see Churston Court, which stands just next door. This is undoubtedly the finest old house in the parish and has great visual charm. It is a homely house with perhaps no aspirations towards grandeur. It is long and low, and of only two storeys in height; but it nestles snugly into its secluded corner with somehow a promise of open hearths and roaring fires with cosy beds and creature comforts by the score.

We should do well to pause a moment in the gateway and consider how for over nine centuries a manorhouse has stood on this site, for Churston – then "Cerceton" – was a Domesday manor. Throughout that long period both church and state have been represented by these two buildings, which stand yet side by side to welcome us. The house is less imposing than many a Devon farmhouse, but displays an array of mullioned windows typical of the fifteenth century, a rounded front door and low, undistinguished chimneys – all done in the local red sandstone and weathered to soft, mellow tones.

It is almost impossible to conjecture what the ground plan of this old house may have been. A pointed doorway gives onto a wing running north. At the end of this an old chimney survives, so this wing may be pre-sixteenth century. The house has been a hotel for some years now; the old rooms have been partitioned and the walls much disturbed over the years. All one can safely assert is that this house in its initial stage was probably a simple hall-house. In its next stage, when the north–south wing was added, it could have become L-shaped. Then thirdly came the intruding Tudor wing of two storeys.

There used to be an excellent staircase of black oak not so long ago and also fine panelling in the principal rooms; but at some period all this was ripped out and no one seems to know where it went. The remaining panelling in the bar looks eighteenth century. So the visitor will understand that, apart from the charming façade, little else remains.

GALMPTON

Galmpton lies on the south-west side of the parish, extending to the river at Galmpton Creek, whilst in the opposite direction it reaches towards Torbay at Galmpton Warborough. "Galmentona" and "Cercetona" were both Domesday manors, and at that time there must have been very definite boundaries between them. It does not seem that there was ever a village beside the church and manor house at Churston Ferrers, for the present village would appear to be entirely of nineteenth century date. It seems pretty clear that the village of Galmpton is where the bulk of the population has always lived – comfortably situated in a sunny fold in the hills, and away from the bitter east wind which howls across the Common. The village has managed to retain its old-world atmosphere whilst at the same time it has absorbed quite a large amount of modern building. Indeed the old and the new somehow manage to blend together at Galmpton – much better than in a lot of villages. There are some attractive cottages and old farm buildings to admire although next door there may be a bungalow. But then the gardens of the modern growth all seem to be exceptionally well tended, and that makes all the difference. This is one of Devon's old villages and a walk round it is well worth while. The hill down to it brings you to The Roundings – a delightfully inapt name for a triangle of roads! Here turn right as for Stoke Gabriel. Keep straight on until the next left turn. This is a pleasant lane which will eventually arrive at the School. A left turn here, where a tall tree makes an unusual traffic island, brings one back to the starting point. This little jaunt is perhaps less than a mile in length but is well worth doing, for it gives such a good idea of the sort of place Galmpton is and of the smiling countryside which surrounds it.

THE CHAPEL OF THE GOOD SHEPHERD

Galmpton folk had to go to Churston Ferrers church in the old days for this was, and still is, their parish church; but it is a tidy step from Galmpton, so when the village expanded, a conveniently placed barn at Vale Farm was purchased and converted into a chapel, which was opened in 1961 and is dedicated to the Good Shepherd. It contains some things of great interest: first, an altar table which is a copy of John Wycliff's ancient altar at Lutterworth; and secondly the reredos, which came from the disused church of St Peter the Fisherman at Brixham. This displays a painting by Mrs Hogg, daughter of the well-known Rev. Henry Lyte, author of the hymn "Abide with me". The third item is the bell, which was presented by the PCC of Upton, Torquay. It had been for some seventy years at St James's, Upton, but when that was converted into a youth centre it was no longer required there. The bell was old, however, when it was presented to St James's in 1891, for it had been the house bell at Torwood Manor – an old Tudor manor house in Torquay which stood a little above the Museum, but was demolished in 1843. Dr Paget Blake, a collector of curios, then acquired it and later presented it to St James's. It bears an eighteenth century inscription, "Humphry Abam Gent W. E. 1739". A full account of the bell is in my book *Upton the Heart of Torquay*. After many vicissitudes it has found a resting place at this attractive little wayside chapel at Galmpton.

GOOSEBERRY PIE

Churston Ferrers and Galmpton have a common bond in their famous Gooseberry Pie. This must surely be first cousin to the traditional Paignton Pudding. The antiquity of both is not to be questioned, for their roots go back time out of mind. An excellent Gooseberry Pie was made in 1951 on June 25th when, according to the local newspaper, there was a revival of the old Gooseberry Pie Feast. In that year there was held throughout the country a "Festival of Britain", when all things to do with the country's traditional culture, art and customs were displayed throughout the land. So that was considered just the time to hold a Pie Festival.

The pie when cooked stood 15 inches high and contained a hundredweight of gooseberries. It was divided into 400 slices which were sold at 9d. each. Well-wishers from as far away as Canada, the USA and Australia sent fats to swell the huge amounts of ingredients needed.

GREENWAY

An attractive country road leads south-westwards from the village and climbs towards Brim Hill, after which a mile-long descent through wooded scenery leads down to the Dart at Greenway where there is a slipway and ferry. Parking here is easy out of season, but in the summer the queue is liable to stretch back towards Galmpton. The ferry crosses to Dittisham, which is picturesquely situated on the opposite bank of the river. It is worth while crossing to see the village, enjoy a pint of scrumpy and visit the fine church of St George. The Dart here is at its widest. Those who are interested in boats will like Greenway, for there are moorings here stretching upriver towards Galmpton Creek.

GALMPTON CREEK

Take the Stoke Gabriel road out of the village and then a left turn at the next signpost. From here a typical meandering Devon lane leads to Galmpton Creek. Take it slowly and enjoy its full flavour, for it's all too short. The visitor should be warned that the Creek is all about boats, and boats are all about the Creek. They crop up in gardens, behind hedges, along roads – indeed everywhere where one can be stowed. On fine days their proud owners are for ever painting them and pondering over them with a deep concern, tempered by dreadful concentration. It struck me that there must be more boats ashore than are ever to be seen on the river! If arriving by car, get rid of it immediately, for you can go no further. Continue walking in the direction in which you have come and the lane you are on will lead steeply upwards. From this hill there are excellent views of the boatyards. Further on there are seductive peeps of the river and the promise of a stroll to Greenway slipway and ferry. If you take the opposite direction the second boatyard is reached, behind which are extensive worked-out quarries. They have been put to the best possible use, for they are choc à bloc with boats! Indeed they seem to be of all sizes, shapes and descriptions. To follow the river upwards here is beautiful but painful because there is no path and the shore is littered with loose stones from the former quarry. In about a quarter of a mile the private estate of Waddeton Court is reached, so this terminates the walk; but before returning take a look at the two very old piers of free-stone walling. They are said to have been built by the Canons of Torre Abbey, who owned a part of Waddeton and constructed fishponds and traps here which still exist. So Galmpton Creek with its boats and broad river is well worth your visit; it is one of Dart Country's most alluring nooks.

MAYPOOL

Maypool is the first of a series of elegant country houses which adorn this bend of the river between Kingswear and Stoke Gabriel. All stand in their own spacious grounds and most have access to the river. After Maypool comes Greenway House, then Waddeton Court, Sandridge Park and Barton, South Downs, Stoke Gabriel House, Woods House and finally Duncannon House.

On the road to Greenway ferry is a left fork; this leads to Maypool, a large Victorian house, yet not in the least resembling the Italianate houses at Kingswear. It is built of a warm red stone surmounted by a red tiled roof. It was built for F. C. Simpson, the engineer, who owned and founded the shipyard at Noss, later known as Philip's shipyard. The foundation stone was laid in 1883 by his son, then aged three.

The architect was Robert Medley Fulford. The house is now an active YHA. It is superbly situated facing right down the river; with its gabled wings and charming arcaded verandah it deserves careful consideration. The interior boasts several things of interest – a large "Gothic" fireplace in the hall, a wooden gallery and a staircase lit from above. In one of the rooms there is a stained glass window containing musical figures. The woodwork is said by Miss Anne Simpson, grand-daughter of F. C. Simpson, to have come from the shipyard just at the time when wood was no longer being required so much in the building of ships. So her grandfather seems to have used up his preponderance of wood in his fine new house. Instead of sailing the seven seas it ended up at Maypool. The house stands on the edge of a steep valley down which there flows an attractive stream; this, as it reaches the river, forms a pleasant ornamental pool.

It comes as a complete surprise, however, to see, spanning the valley, one of Brunel's spectacular railway viaducts of seven arches, which in style and composition resembles its contemporary at Broadsands. In winter, when there is no foliage on the trees, a stretch of the railway can be seen climbing through the woods beside the river as it approaches Greenway tunnel, which is just beyond the viaduct.

GREENWAY HOUSE

The next of the riverside houses is Greenway House. On the way down to the ferry its gates are to be seen on the left. The gardens are occasionally open to the public but the house is private. It has ancient roots, and the ruined shell of a Tudor house is still to be seen in the grounds. Here Humphrey Gilbert was born c.1539. The present house is

Georgian and was built around 1780. It consists of five bays, a porch and a parapet. It is of interest today because Dame Agatha Christie lived and worked here to the time of her death in 1976. Greenway was the setting for her novel *Deadman's Folly*, and it was in the boathouse here that the murdered girl was found. It was a clever plot, the murderer, as usual, being quite unsuspected until the last chapter, when Hercule Poirot solves everything.

LUPTON HOUSE

Lupton House, which stands on the Torbay side of the ridge of hills between Churston Ferrers and the river, has in its day been a well-situated country mansion. It stands in spacious grounds and is approached by a well-wooded drive. Once it was an elegant Palladian house and was built for Charles Hayne, who was Sheriff of Devon in 1772. In 1840 Sir J. B. Yarde Buller had it remodelled, and in 1862 Salvin, the famous architect, did further work which was later demolished. Then in 1926 a disastrous fire occurred which gutted most of the house. The rebuilding did not include the second floor. So today there remains a house in excellent Georgian style on two sides only, for the other two are featureless. The front door, originally at the front of the house, is now at the side, and the magnificent porte-cochère, which once existed, is no more.

The house is now Gramercy Hall School. One cannot help but think the scholars fortunate who work in these stately surroundings. The entrance to the drive is much enhanced by the two day-lodges with their attractive Doric pilasters and pediments.

Another charming lodge for your camera stands at the entrance to Lupton Park. On the road up to Hillhead it is on the left. Opposite are stables, and beneath the gable don't miss seeing the fine beagle's head. Lupton Park is a nicely situated modern house by Oswald Milne.

BROADSANDS DOLMEN – AN ASTONISHING SURVIVAL

In one of the few surviving fields between Broadsands and the railway you may stumble upon a prehistoric dolmen or chambered tomb. The site was, and to some extent still is, secluded; but it does seem remarkable that it had never been recognised for what it is until 1957, when Guy Belville, a keen amateur archaeologist who had recently settled in a house nearby, brought it to the attention of the Devon Archaeological Exploration Society. The name of the field south of the monument is Shilstone, meaning "shelfstone", according to the tithe map of Churston Ferrers (1839). This exactly describes the huge shelf-like stone which once capped the dolmen, but which has long ago slipped off its supporters and lies in a semi-recumbent position. The dolmen is to some extent camouflaged by the stony hedgerow on which it lies. This is also of some antiquity, for it forms the ancient boundary between Paignton and Churston Ferrers.

In 1958 an excavation was carried out by the DAES under Dr C. A. Ralegh Radford. It was discovered that a mound had originally covered the dolmen, which proved to be a small chambered tomb approached by a passage. In style it resembled tombs which are found in the Iberian Peninsula and NW France. Human bones, some pottery and the ashes of ritual fires were discovered. Such tombs belong to the Neolithic period, though no definite date was assigned to the Broadsands tomb. A comprehensive report on the excavation will be found in the *Proceedings* for 1957/8 of the DAES, volume 5, parts 5 and 6, where there is an article by Dr Radford.

STOKE GABRIEL

Stoke Gabriel is a very bright jewel in the crown of Dart Country. Situated at the head of a creek, the village is joined to the River Dart, yet separated from it by the length of the very entry which leads to it. Moreover, it has its own rival attraction – a very alluring pond half a mile long and bounded by hills which are graced on the one side by green fields and on the other by abundant woods. This was once a millpond. What a place it is to visit on a summer's day, with the water glistening in the strong light and ripples gaily dancing as the breeze stirs the water into life! It is a place quite unlike anywhere else, for here you can sit all day by the pond and never tire, just relaxing in the sunshine. When you have feasted your eyes on the pond and its surroundings you can turn your gaze in the other direction to admire the peep of the river in the distance; or, if it's low tide, take

a stroll beside the quay and consider fishing nets put out to dry, or the tasty delicacy of a Dart salmon which may come your way. This attractive quay is quite cut off from the village and seems a place apart – a little world of beauty all on its own. The strange thing is that as soon as the short hill to the village is undertaken then it is no longer to be seen, except perhaps from the windows of the houses on the hill. The village has retained much of its old-world character. Consider Church Walk, for instance, which begins with the Church House Inn and continues with a row of old houses which includes the first schoolroom of the village – all this has an atmosphere of bygone days. It ends most appropriately at the church, which is, of course, the most interesting building; but there is throughout the village a good sprinkling of old houses and cottages, all in fine condition, their varied chimneys adding much to the general interest of the buildings. Don't miss seeing Barnhay – a delightful cul de sac behind the Castle and much beloved of artists. Everything, you will find, is extremely bright and smiling.

There are three pubs where you may regale yourself; but no longer on good old scrumpy, I fear. The old orchards which produced the apples have had their day; so you will have to go elsewhere for your scrumpy.

The first pub you will see is the Castle, which has a fine site on the highest point of the old village. It is an early nineteenth century Gothic type of building with very solid castellations, and was first built as a vicarage. Just below stands the venerable Church House Inn, which one can believe goes right back to mediaeval times. The bar contains a large hearth and a profusion of moulded beams. The story goes that from beneath its roof it was once possible to crawl beneath all the roofs in Church Walk and make your escape into the churchyard, and so quickly away by boat on a high tide. So if you were a wanted man Stoke Gabriel treated you kindly. The story is a good one and you don't have to believe it – I think a local paper was my source. At the bottom of the hill stands the Victoria and Albert – its name being reflected in its appearance and charming situation.

A little above it, and on the other side of the hill, is a fine house of the same period with an attractive tower. This was Hill House, the residence of the last squire. It is now Gabriel Court Hotel. Below this, and on the opposite side of the road stands Stoke House, a very atmospheric old building with a Georgian frontage; but there is somehow a feeling that its core may be very much older than that. Close by are old farmhouses and it could well be that here, down in the dip, is the oldest part of the village.

Had you visited the village in the early twentieth century you would have been struck by the number of people employed in salmon fishing, for here the very best Dart salmon is to be found. Now, however, much less fishing goes on. I was assured by an octogenarian fisherman that there is no one getting a living entirely by fishing now. This is due to pollution and other causes. But the industry survives yet as a hobby and interest in it seems to run in families. If you have time, you will not be wasting it by exploring the maze of old lanes which surround the village. These make for pleasant, traffic-free walking. They are full of surprises, and you may find here an old well, and there a nicely constructed limekiln or a quarry, where a century ago there was much activity. Woods House and the old vicarage are beautifully built houses, all the stone coming from these local limestone quarries. In the lanes one feels miles away from anywhere, yet all the time the great sprawl of Torbay is only two miles away. So enjoy this remnant of fast-vanishing countryside whilst you may.

THE CHURCH OF ST MARY AND ST GABRIEL

Only a few feet above the millpond is the fine old church of St Mary and St Gabriel. The tapering tower dominates the scene. It is a bold tower, 65 feet in height and containing a melodious ring of six bells. It is by far the oldest part of the church, and a thirteenth century date is generally assigned to it, whilst the rest of the building was reconstructed in the fifteenth century. The most ornate part of the exterior is the cunningly wrought north doorway, which forms such a perfect ending to the vista along Church Walk and the churchyard path. So after pausing to examine the quite sumptuous carving round the door, we enter the church with a feeling of expectation which is well rewarded by a spacious and lofty interior. Judged by Devonshire standards the building is extremely lofty for its length, and this feeling of uplift is enhanced by the tall pillars of white Beer stone, whose capitals are so delicately worked. Look out for Jock o'the Green, that pagan spirit of the woods which the old masons so delighted to portray. A most sophisticated version of Jock appears on the capital nearest the door, with foliage issuing from his mouth.

The church still retains its elaborate fifteenth century rood screen, which has been well restored by Herbert Read of Exeter. In the wainscoting are the painted figures of saints and prophets. The elaborately carved pulpit is of the same period. Here the carving is rich and beautiful, but the niches still await the replacement of those images of saints which must once have adorned them. The font will also date from the same period as the screen and pulpit. It is octagonal and of local stone; at the base are traces of mediaeval colour.

Among the lesser lovely things are the excellent wall tablets and memorials of which there are quite a number. They are of all sizes, shapes and styles, dating from the late seventeenth century to the twentieth. They are worth careful study. Only three of the old fifteenth century pews survive, but note the unusual arrangement of box pews with poppyheads and doors in the south aisle. Were they reserved for the gentry, I wonder?

Carefully preserved, and still in situ, are the oil lamps of a former day – not hanging from the arcade as was most usual, but mounted on standards. Somehow they managed to survive when electricity first came along. Now they are treasured and lit once a year for the Service of the Nine Lessons and Carols.

Other survivals (in a glass case at the end of the north aisle) are a *Book of Homilies* (1683), Foxe's *Book of Martyrs*, a Black Letter Bible and a "Vinegar Bible". In the latter the word "vinegar" was inserted instead of "vineyard" in St Luke's Gospel. On the south wall is a coat of arms of Queen Anne.

The church plate has amongst other items an Elizabethan chalice and two pieces of Queen Anne's reign given by the Pomeroys of Sandridge. The south chapel was the perquisite of this family, whilst the north chapel belonged to whatever family was residing at Waddeton Court.

The churchyard is a wonderful place to sit and rest on a summer's day, for the views from there are superb. Just below Church Walk, in a preserved orchard, there are seats where you can do

just this, and drink in the beauties around. The most noteworthy feature of the churchyard is the magnificent yew tree, which is said to be one of the oldest in the country. Its age is assessed at between 800 and 1,000 years. It has a spread of thirty feet and its branches are supported on crutches. In the folklore attached to it, to get your wish, you must walk round it three times backwards, just as at Berry Pomeroy Castle, but there, to do it properly, you must be blindfold as well!

STOKE GABRIEL IN THE DOMESDAY BOOK

"It was in Domesday", they say, as they refer to an old barn or pig sty; but of course it never was! Yet some people seem to have the greatest faith in the antiquity of certain things around them. Indeed "Domesday" is credited with a mass of items of which its innocent pages never dreamed. So it's often rather fun to try to separate the wheat from the chaff where the great Survey of 1087 is concerned. Because there are three manors with the name of "Stoche" or "Stoch" in Domesday, writers have never paused to differentiate between them. One seems to have adopted the manor mentioned on page 735 of the old nineteenth century version of Domesday, and this has been copied by one writer after another, and so the mistake (if mistake it be) proliferates. Now I prefer the "Stoche" mentioned on page 111, where there is mention of the Bishop of Exeter as lord of the manor, and also of two mills. In support of this the historian Hugh Watkin, on page 51 of "Transactions of the Devonshire Association (1932)" says "the lordship of the manor of Stoke Gabriel was always held by the lord of the manor of Paignton", i.e. the Bishop. As for the two mills, everyone in the village knows that there were formerly two at Stoke Gabriel. Byter Mill, which is of decided antiquity, still stands, whilst there is photographic evidence of the former tidal mill which once stood at the opposite end of the pond. There is no difficulty in believing that they were clacking away merrily at the time of Domesday.

There were three other sub-manors in the parish – Aish, Waddeton and Sandridge. The last two were not Domesday manors, but Aish is there all right; and yet this is the one which so far no writer has mentioned. This delightful little hamlet is just the sort of small independent community which even today looks as though it would have been a manor in its own right. It appears in Domesday as "Aisse", and I choose it among other manors of the same name because no less a person than Radulf de Pomerai was its lord. Again we have a close neighbour, with his manor of Berry Pomeroy abutting on Aisse. So I do feel it right to include Aisse as a sub-manor of Stoke Gabriel on its proximity to Berry Pomeroy alone.

THE TWO MILLS OF STOKE GABRIEL

The Domesday evidence establishes that at the time there were two mills in the manor and these stood, I have no doubt, at Byter and at the foot of the pond. No one in 800 years has come up with alternative sites, and for geographical reasons I don't think they ever will, so let us consider Byter Mill first. The approach road from the village is by means of a secluded lane which wends its way on a high bank beside the pond. This is followed to its head, and a pleasant walk it is, through a forest of trees of varied species, with glimpses of the pond here and there. Owing to subsidence of the bank of the pond the lane is now a cul de sac, so with traffic at a minimum this makes an ideal walk for dogs. It is perhaps at its best in early summer when the fresh verdure of the trees is at its height. At the mill the road is open to traffic coming down from Port Bridge.

The buildings at Byter Mill are enclosed behind a high wall, like so many of the local farmhouses. This surrounds a large yard on two sides with the millhouse and stream on the other two, thus making an impressive enclosure. The millhouse is of three storeys and may well date from the eighteenth century. In the yard there stands a large granite millstone, but the wheel has disintegrated, though its position at the side of the house is easy to determine. In time of spate the stream is very active and a fine sight as it tumbles down in a turbulent cascade over stone steps. Altogether this is a picturesque spot where the abundant trees play their part.

The other mill was a tidal mill, and a much more exciting proposition. Such mills, strange to say, were by no means common in Devon. I am told that in the nineteenth century only twenty-five existed, whilst today there are none. By great good luck a photograph of the mill at Stoke Gabriel still exists. It shows the mill to have been a really old building. It looks to have been built on a sandy bar and occupied, so I am told, a site just about where the shop and toilets on the quay stand today. Its waterwheel in the photo can be clearly distinguished on the south side. Some yards further towards the shore stood the millhouse. Both buildings from their dimensions look to be of mediaeval origin.

DUNCANNON

Don't miss visiting Duncannon. This is a beauty spot on a bend in the river upstream from the village. It has its own beach and jetty and is yet another splendid place to idle away an hour or so in the summer warmth, and if you're lucky you may see the salmon fishers pulling in their nets to examine their sparkling catch. Duncannon is situated about half a mile from the village – anyone will tell you which lane to take. This particular one is narrow, and I seem to remember that cars are not permitted along it. It is well above the river and affords some pleasant views of it. At its entrance there stands Stoke Gabriel House, which is one of the fine houses gracing the river bank just here, standing amid secluded gardens and imposing outbuildings. It presents a façade of many windows, the unusual pattern of whose window-bars is of decided interest. There is also an imposing porch.

Duncannon House, lower down and close to the river, is a another good house of the same period. Attractive as these stately Georgian homes may be, the modern houses on the left at the beginning of the lane are worth a second glance, for they are well spread out beside a road with wide grass verges trimly mown. An excellent piece of planning this; why can't it always be done as well?

Above Duncannon and commanding splendid views of the river is Woods House. Its foundation stone bears the date 1897; it is thus a late Victorian house with a frontage which displays two graceful gables which are slate-hung. At the rear are older farm buildings which suggest that the present house succeeds a much older farmhouse. Before the front door is an interesting relic of former days – a nicely made four-sided direction post of which this is the top. It is of sandstone and bears letters on its four faces – D (Dartmouth), T (Totnes), P (Paignton) and N (Newton Abbot). The puzzle of course is to find the crossroads where it once stood. Not very far off I should think.

SOUTH DOWNS

Just below Byter Mill is a bridge over the millstream; the road which it carries leads through a long and well-wooded drive to South Downs – one of the riverside houses which commands excellent views of the river. It is a well-built Victorian house standing on a high bank above older farm buildings.

AISH

There is a delightfully situated hamlet one mile NW of the village, and quite lost among the hills. This is Aish – pronounced Ash. Here on the sunny slope of a steep hill there stand a farmhouse or two, a cottage or two, and best of all, two large and imposing Georgian-style houses. Aish Cross House (built 1815), as its name implies, is at the cross roads at the top of the hill. It has an intriguing turret and fine fenestration and stands amid a secluded walled garden. Just below it, and on the opposite side of the road, is Aish House – a very dignified building with a frontage of five bays and a fine porch. The excellent fenestration is in its original state. Particularly attractive is the circular window within the gable. There is good plasterwork inside, and the vaulting in the entrance hall is a pleasant surprise. The house stands amid well-kept lawns at the top of a rise. Both houses are private.

If you want to see two fine old farmhouses, turn right at the crossroads and you will soon reach Bowhay and, just beyond it, Higher Aish, which has its venerable old farm buildings still intact.

Aish is a delightful little entity in itself, much resembling Waddeton on the other side of Stoke Gabriel which we shall soon be considering.

SANDRIDGE PARK

Turning now to the side of the parish which lies south-east of Port Bridge, we reach another of the fine riverside mansions. This is Sandridge Park, which stands in solitary grandeur on the summit of a low hill. It is an imposing early nineteenth century mansion designed in 1805 by the celebrated architect Nash in a most exuberant style. It is indeed a whimsical building with elliptical towers and oval windows. It commands magnificent vistas of the river which, just below Galmpton Creek, is at its widest. Sandridge Park was built for the widow of the second Lord Ashburton; she was succeeded by Lord Cranston.

Adjoining the house is a fine indoor swimming pool, the interesting thing being that the block which contains it is designed in impeccable Georgian style with rounded windows. This adjunct is so cleverly contrived that it almost appears a part of the house itself. Pevsner in *The Buildings of England – Devon* expressed himself delighted with the restoration of the stables and the way they have been converted to other uses.

It is stated in quite a few places that John Davis, the celebrated Elizabethan navigator and globe-trotter, was born here at an older house on the same site. This, however, is now generally considered wrong, and it is thought that Davis was born at Sandridge Barton which stands not far away down the hill to the south-east. Whether Nash's house succeeded an older one is debatable, for no old buildings of any kind appear there now. It is much more probable that the ruin of the large house above the farmyard at Sandridge Barton is the predecessor of Sandridge Park.

SANDRIDGE BARTON

The array of old buildings at Sandridge Barton form an interesting group. The oldest thing there, however, is not a building at all but the gigantic trunk of an elm tree which must be many centuries old, rivalling its sister in Stoke Gabriel churchyard. This tree is now unfortunately dead – its trunk in the very last stages of decay. But its great girth, said to be 44 feet, can still be appreciated. When I first saw the tree, c. 1960, it stood to a height of about 12 feet and stunted branches still grew from the old trunk. Most exciting of all was a door in its side. Opening this revealed an active stream bubbling up in the centre of the trunk and flowing away beneath. The trunk was quite hollow. It is probable that there would be a stone shelf here at one time. So it could have been used as a butter cooler – the forerunner of the modern fridge.

The farm buildings stand in a dip in the hills and facing the river. The oldest, which is situated higher than the rest, must be the old manor house of Sandridge. It is a large house, much overgrown, but this does not hinder one from seeing that it was a house of standing. It would be where Adrian Gilbert came to live when he left Greenway, and later the Pomeroys. It often happens in Devon that the barton house is quite near the manor house, and this seems to have been a case in point, for the barton house is only a few yards below the old ruin. The house is in fine condition and appears Georgian. Nevertheless it is considered to be part Tudor. But whatever its date let us respect it, for John Davis was more probably born here than anywhere else, and would have had his first encounter with boats and their ways in the river below.

The farmyard has been modernised, but two interesting vernacular buildings remain: (1) a shippen with tall, circular columns punctuating the walls, and (2) a hay barn constructed on eight circular columns, but with a raised floor. The pillars wear stone collars, evidently to prevent rats from climbing up to the granary floor.

There are early mentions of "Sandrigge" in 1238 and "Sanderig" in 1242. It was a sub-manor in Stoke Gabriel, but I can find no mention of it in Domesday, so it must have come into being as a manor after 1087. Sandridge and Waddeton were the leading houses in the parish, so it is not surprising that the south and north chapels in the church were appropriated by them respectively.

To hikers it must seem unfortunate that, unlike most of the coastline, the banks of the Dart are privately owned, and so those who wish to walk from Kingswear to Totnes just cannot do it. Below Sandridge at Ladies Quay, there seems to be much of interest. Listen to what Hemery has to say of it in *Historic Dart* – "The woodland path leads straight to an artificial cutting through rock some twenty feet high to a small beach which it approaches over steep, flat rock bedding. If ever there was a place for a clandestine landing of some thing or body, this is it". He goes on to say that the cutting is wide enough for a pack of animals to pass and enquires what stories the rocks of Ladies Quay secrete.

THE TWO FAMOUS SONS OF STOKE GABRIEL

Stoke Gabriel has in its time produced two famous sons and the earliest of these was John Davis of Sandridge who was born here c. 1550. He sailed further north than had ever been done before in his attempt to find the north-west passage. This, of course, was not where he expected and he explored instead the quite unknown coast of Greenland. As Arthur Mee says in *Devon*, "he revealed the wealth of the Arctic and New World in whales and fish, and created an industry which enriched the nation and bred a race of mariners and explorers unmatched in skill and hardihood. In his track sailed the men who were to found our Western Empire". On his last voyage, in the East, he was treacherously murdered by pirates whom he had just rescued.

The diary which Davis kept on his Arctic voyage became the model for the logbook system which ships have kept ever since. After his Arctic explorations he undertook many other voyages in various parts of the world. His navigational instruments were still in use many years after his death.

GEORGE JACKSON CHURCHWARD

In the course of time Stoke Gabriel produced another famous son, and this was George Jackson Churchward, who came from a long-established village family and was born at Rowe's Farm in 1857. He was from his early days a railway enthusiast. He would, as a nipper, have remembered well the excitement in the district when the Kingswear line was opened in 1864. He worked in the maintenance sheds at Newton Abbot from the age of sixteen, and from this humble beginning he rose to the top of the engineering side of the GWR. He was Chief Mechanical Engineer at Swindon from 1902 to 1921. During this period he designed several famous classes of engines including the "Great Bear", Britain's first Pacific 4-6-2 class. An engine of the famous Castle class was called after him. So highly was he esteemed at Swindon that he became at one time Mayor of the town.

George's death was a sad one, for he was killed on the line one foggy morning whilst walking between two trains. It is strange that he who was so enthralled by railways should have been brought up in a parish where no railway ever ran. But doubtless, as a boy, he often walked the three miles to Churston station just to watch the engines shunting and wait to see the London train come steaming proudly in.

STOKE GABRIEL COUNTY PRIMARY SCHOOL

Along Church Walk, and above the Verger's Cottage, is the old schoolroom of the village which is said to date from 1642. The present excellent school building dates from 1876. Stoke Gabriel County Primary School began as a National School in 1839. Then in 1876 it became a Board School and is now a County Primary School. If compared with the usual heavy buildings of its period this is a little gem. Who was the architect, I wonder? It stands part way up the hill, where it looks most attractive with its headmaster's house, tower and clock – to say nothing of a pyramid with a weathervane!

WADDETON

Above the bank of the river, and just above Galmpton Creek lies a snugly situated hamlet. This is Waddeton (pronounced Watton), and until quite recently it consisted only of a manor house and a few cottages. Now, however, you will find that a little more has been added to it. Nevertheless nothing has been done to spoil the peace of this rural retreat – indeed with the "Big House" and its stately entrance so prominent on the skyline, one can say that the feeling is still positively feudal. "Wadeton" is mentioned as a manor quite early, but it is not in Domesday. Its lord was always the Bishop of Exeter, like Paignton and Stoke Gabriel. In 1199 it was "Wadenton".

Not far from the entrance to Waddeton Court, and on the left-hand side, stands the chapel. It is of red sandstone and dedicated to St Michael. It is generally accepted that it was built about the middle of the thirteenth century. In 1868 it was rebuilt on the old site, but it is difficult to believe that much of the old fabric was retained. A hexagonal apse was added, and this is the salient feature of the interior. There are two small windows to each face, filled with the stained glass of the period, and the effect is unusual. A most attractive feature of the chancel is the excellent brass candelabrum. There are memorials to the Studdy and Goodson

families and one to Roy Neville Craig, in his day a prominent Torquay doctor. On the south wall of the chancel Eleanor Holdsworth "who restored this oratory" is commemorated. The present Waddeton Court is a solidly built house of the Tudor style commanding exquisite views of the river. The architect was Thomas Lidstone, who later restored Kingswear Castle. A splendid relic of the former manor house has survived and is to be seen at Torquay Museum; this is a carved series of wooden figures representing the "Nine Worthies", who are mentioned by Shakespeare in *Love's Labours Lost* and by Mallory in *La Morte d'Arthur*. They are said to have been in the dining room.

Beside the chapel is a pleasant lawn on which stands the ruined entrance door once attached to the old manor house. Behind it, and at a lower level than the chapel, are the ruins of an extensive house, evidently the forerunner of Waddeton Court. Before the doorway there stand a late eighteenth century cannon and a wooden buoy in a metal frame. Both were at some time retrieved from the river.

EARTHWORK ON BASELY COMMON

Lower Well Farm (mentioned 1242) is one of the old holdings of the parish. There is a fine barn still remaining here, and the house, with its two old chimneys, by its very shape suggests a longhouse. The walls are covered in stucco, so it is not possible to see if they are of cob or stone. On the summit of Basely Common, which is the hill to the east, there is, however, a far older holding – doubtless the forerunner of the present farm. Here, on the skyline as you climb up from below, stand the low, worn-down banks of a quadrangular earthwork some 100 feet across. An excavation took place here during the years 1958–60 under Ted Masson Phillips of Totnes. His opinion was that this was a Romano-British homestead dating from about the first century AD. Within the area is a small building – probably a house – and there were postholes for supporting timbers for walls and roofs. There were surface finds of Roman ware of the second and third centuries AD, and a bronze brooch and coins of the fourth century. There is a well-defined entrance to the south, and there were traces of more fields and banks outside the enclosure.

Roman pottery and shells were found in 1959 in a village garden at Stoke Gabriel, indicating that the Romans were visitors, if not settlers there. They would have penetrated by sea and river, rather than overland.

Even if you are no archaeologist it is well worth climbing the hill for the view alone. Here, spread out before you is all the wonderful countryside between Stoke Gabriel and Dartmoor, with the twisting river valley weaving its way through the hills on your left.

All this, on a clear day, is a never-to be-forgotten sight; so now that we have come to the end of our tour of Dart Country, let's sit down and rest awhile. "What's in the rucksack, Joe?"